DISCOVERING DINOSAURS

Written by Myka-Lynne Sokoloff
Illustrated by Greg Harris

Sadlier-Oxford
A Division of William H. Sadlier, Inc.
New York, NY 10005-1002

Barosaurus

Irsosaurus

Elaphrosaurus

Have you ever seen a dinosaur? Maybe you've seen one in a museum or on the pages of a book. But no one has ever seen a living dinosaur.

2

Brachiosaurus

Stegosaurus

Dinosaurs lived millions of years ago.
They came in all shapes and sizes—
some even had spikes. Yikes!

Until about 200 years ago, no one knew about dinosaurs. Then people began finding clues in stone. They found teeth, bones, eggs, and prints of dinosaurs. These clues are called fossils.

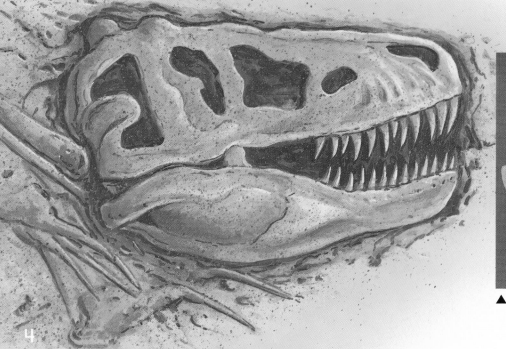

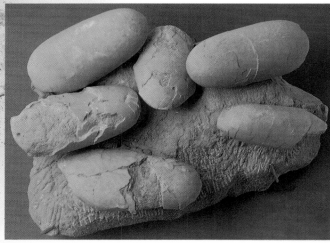

▲ Fossilized dinosaur eggs

◄ Fossilized footprint of T-Rex

▲ Digging up fossilized bones

People who look for fossils are called paleontologists. They use fossils to make guesses about what dinosaurs looked like and how they lived.

5

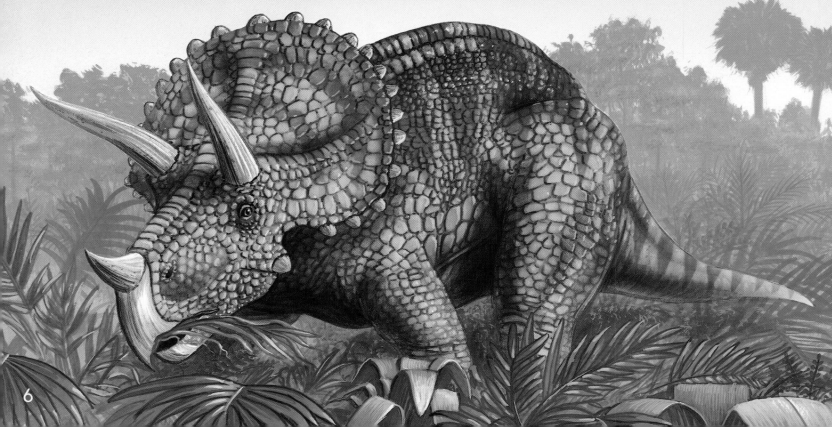

Today experts know when dinosaurs lived. They also know that some dinosaurs ate plants and others ate animals.

MEAT-EATERS

Most meat-eaters stood and moved on their two back legs. That way they could run fast and catch other animals.

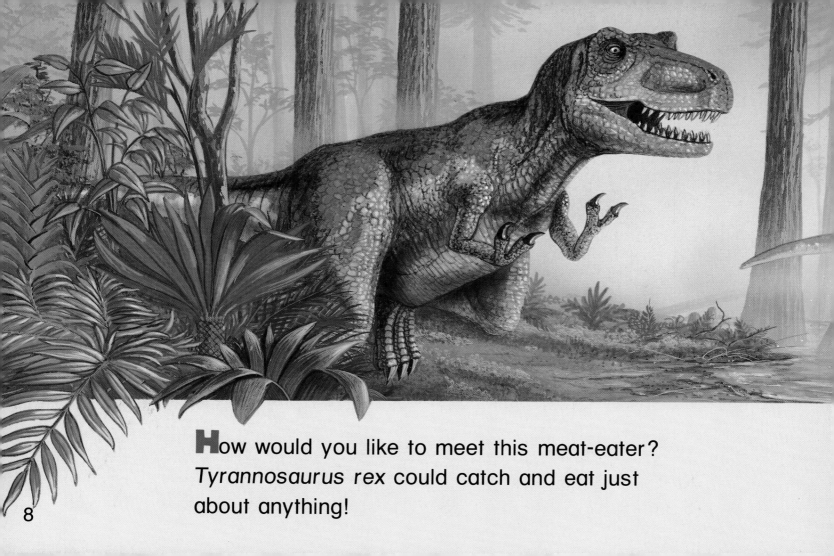

How would you like to meet this meat-eater?
Tyrannosaurus rex could catch and eat just
about anything!

Tyrannosaurus had very strong jaws and teeth up to 7 inches long. It's likely that T-rex often dined on duck-billed dinosaurs.

Some meat-eaters were small.
Velociraptors were speedy little meat-eaters
that hunted plant-eaters up to five
times their own size!

10

Some of the biggest dinosaurs that ever lived ate only plants! One group of plant-eaters had bodies with small heads, long necks, long tails, and legs like tree trunks.

11

Plant-eaters often moved on all fours.
They may have munched on some plants
that grew in lakes and swamps.

No plants were out of reach for a hungry
Barosaurus—the tallest dinosaur of them all.
It could reach treetops as high as a building
five stories tall!

Fossils show that many plant-eaters
lived in small herds and fed together.
Living in herds helped to keep them
safe from meat-eaters.

What else can you dig up on dinosaurs?
Tell your friends what you find out!

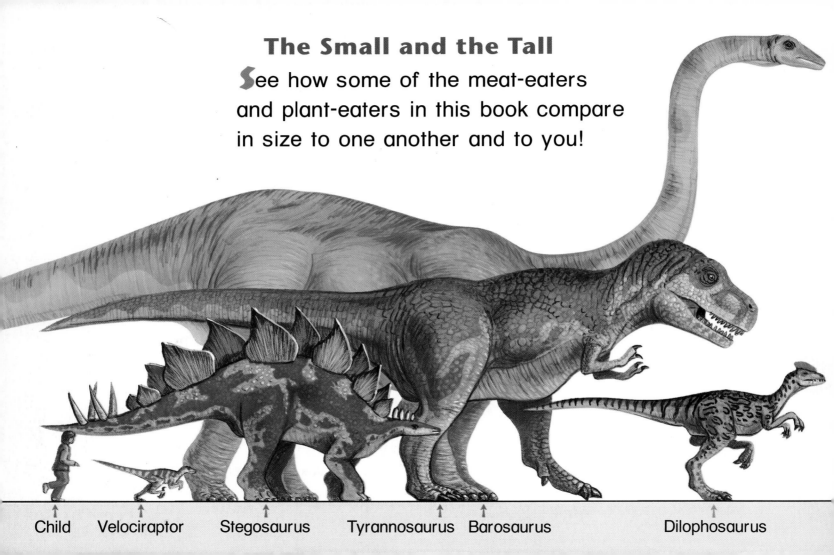

The Small and the Tall

See how some of the meat-eaters and plant-eaters in this book compare in size to one another and to you!

Child Velociraptor Stegosaurus Tyrannosaurus Barosaurus Dilophosaurus